[1001] photographs [1001] photographs [1001] photographs [1001] photographs

[1001] photographs [1001] photographs [1001] photographs [1001] photographs

[1001] photographs [1001] photographs [1001] photographs [1001] photographs

[1001] photographs [1001] photographs [1001] photographs [1001] photographs

[1001] photographs [1001] photographs [1001] photographs [1001] photographs

[1001] photographs [1001] photographs [1001] photographs [1001] photographs

Cats
[1001]
[photos]

© 2007 Rebo International b.v., Lisse, the Netherlands

www.rebo-publishers.com
info@rebo-publishers.com

Text: Françoise Huart and Ségolène Roy
Photography: Yves Lanceau and furrytails.nl
Co-ordination: Isabelle Raimond
Graphic design: Gwénaël Le Cossec
Original title: Les Chiens 1001 photos
© 2006 Copyright SA, 12, Villa de Loucine, 75014, Paris, France
Translation: First Edition Translations Ltd, Cambridge, UK
Typesetting: A. R. Garamond s.r.o., Prague, Czech Republic

ISBN 978-90-366-2250-9

Cats
[1001]
photos

REBO
PUBLISHERS

Contents

Shorthaired Cats

Semi-longhaired Cats

Persians

The World of the Cat

Shorthaired
Cats

The Abyssinian takes pride of place in the pantheon of cats. For many people, it represents the most perfect and most demanding of cats, the ultimate symbol of their poise and elegance.

Its astonishing resemblance to the incense-hazed image of the cat goddess Bastet, depicted as proud and solemn in many ancient Egyptian tombs, gives it a mythical identity. This most sought-after and revered cat is the subject of controversy as to its origin. Did it really come from the shores of the Indian Ocean, as some claim, or is it in fact of purely English descent, as others suggest? The most commonly cited African trail is, however, the most probable. But doubt still exists. Was it imported from Abyssinia in the middle of the nineteenth century by a group of British soldiers, or by an admiring British diplomat? Was it perhaps an accidental cross between an Ethiopian cat and ginger and silver tabbies from the United Kingdom?

Abyssinian

Whatever its origin, this cat, with its characteristic "ticking" (each individual hair has a number of bands of darker color), light at the roots, darker at the tips, is striking for its proud demeanor and the aristocratic, almost arrogant charm of its attractive personality.

This intelligent, inquisitive, independent animal is superbly athletic. It is agile and strong, and loves to play, climb, and hunt. Moreover, it is totally, passionately, not to mention exclusively, devoted to its owner. This enigmatic, regal cat summons up all kinds of fantasies. It is a companion that inspires meditation and reverie.

The fine, triangular head of the Abyssinian is held on a long, supple, elegant neck.

The Abyssinian is a superb athlete and is very agile. It adores climbing trees.

The mysterious and elegant Abyssinian seems to be guarding an age-old secret.

There are various types of Abyssinian. The usual one, and the most commonly occurring, has an even brown coat.

The Abyssinian, which needs to be close to nature, may well develop feelings of boredom and desolation if it has to stay indoors too long.

15

The Abyssinian is a great hunter and is very active. It therefore needs a lot of space, and can only really flourish in the outdoors.

Its piercing gaze and proud demeanor make the Abyssinian one of the most beautiful of all pedigree cats.

Its delicate yet strong paws and its long, thin tail help make the Abyssinian the very embodiment of feline grace.

Lakewood, California, 1981: Joe and Grace take in a stray cat, which they call Shulamith. At first, the couple pay little attention to an astounding detail: the unusual nature of Shulamith's ears.

One day she gives birth to four kittens. Joe and Grace then realize that two of them have remarkable curled ears just like their mother. An expert explains to Joe and Grace that this is not a deformity, but a genetic mutation. A new breed of cat has appeared: the American Curl. The "cat with curled ears" or the "cat with crescent ears"—there is no shortage of phrases used to describe this lovely, inquisitive cat, which still commands a high price when sold. (This kind of cat is very rare, with only around 3,000 in the whole world.) Despite its rough, crinkly coat, the American Wirehair has a group of devotees who adore it passionately. The exemplary disposition of this coarse-haired American breed works only in its favor, and its typically curious and affectionate behavior has secured it a place amongt the most good-natured of the companion cats.

The American Shorthair is a cat found all over North America. The Pilgrim Fathers brought these animals to the New World on board the Mayflower to catch rats on the ship. It is now regarded as the national cat, and is in fact the equivalent, because it is the descendant, of the European Shorthair.

American Curl, American Wirehair, and American Shorthair

The American Shorthair can be regarded as a "purebred" version of the ordinary domestic cat.

The American Shorthair is strikingly robust, with great stamina.

The energetic, effervescent intelligence of the American Wirehair is magnificently reflected in its beautiful large, round eyes, which are bright and mocking.

The Russian Blue seems to have come straight out of a novel by Tolstoy or Turgenev. Does this cat, in addition to its beauty, have a Slavonic soul?

Russian Blue

Distinction, dignity, elegance... There are plenty of flattering descriptions for the Russian Blue. It has won the love and admiration of the most fervent of cat enthusiasts, with its inspiring, captivating beauty.

Its different names add to its mystique. In addition to Russian Blue, it is also sometimes called the Maltese Cat, the Blue Archangel, the Archangel Cat, and the Spanish Blue. Its (disputed) history makes reference to a mythical past, a bygone age: in the nineteenth century, sailors from the Russian port of Archangel on the White Sea are supposed to have brought it to England, where rigorous and selective breeding did much to perfect its appearance. Tsar Nicholas II is said to have harbored an inordinate passion for this animal, and the entire aristocracy of his time followed his lead.

Its meow is almost inaudible, from which comes its reputation as the silent cat. In addition to its physical nobility, one of its most famed qualities is its total serenity. The Russian Blue is exceedingly calm; it seems to know no stress or fear. It is an ideal house cat: it likes to be indoors, and loves the peaceful, agreeable comforts of domestic life. It becomes very attached to children, provided they respect its quiet nature and do not treat it too roughly. It is affectionate and true to its owner, and its presence lends the home a cheerful and refined atmosphere.

The short-haired coat with which nature has wisely provided it is woolly and silky, and protects it superbly well from severe cold. The blue color of its coat, with its silvery sheen, like some celestial light, sets off its pale emerald eyes wonderfully.

The Rossian Blue's incomparably elegant, svelte body with its tapering tail makes it a particularly aesthetic cat.

Its large, pointed ears stand up above a broad head on a long, elegant neck.

35

Russian Blue kittens are sometimes undisciplined and playful, despite their calm temperament.

Russian Blues' emerald-green, almond-shaped eyes are exceptionally bright and shiny.

39

The Japanese Bobtail, which was probably imported into Japan over a thousand years ago from China or Korea, has left its impression on innumerable statues, artifacts, prints, engravings, and writings, over the centuries.

It is usually depicted with one paw raised, as if in greeting. This protector of sailors was revered in Japan as a god, and symbolized good fortune and wealth. A mascot of emperors and nobility, it has been bred in the United States since 1968. The Bobtail has a very unusual, characteristic tail, the result of a mutation long ago. It is curved, angled, and kinked, sometimes like a pom-pom or a "bunny tail," and this tail is what gives the Bobtail its nickname of "chrysanthemum cat," after the flower that it resembles. True to its name of Bobtail, the tail is only 2 to 2 3/4 inches (5 to 7 cm) long. If stretched out, however, it would measure 4 to 4 3/4 inches (10 to 12 cm). This strong, slim, elegantly proportioned cat radiates an impression of sinuosity and light. The high cheekbones and broad jaw accentuate the eyes, the color of which depends on the color of the coat.

The steely character of the Bobtail sometimes leads to conflict with other cats. However, it is the ideal cat for a family: friendly and gentle toward children, affectionate and loyal to its owner. Its insatiable curiosity makes it a charming and cheerful companion, which loves to romp and play.

It meows a lot less loudly and frequently than, for instance, the Siamese, but it does not hesitate to announce its presence with its sweet, melodious mewing. It is both an indoor and an outdoor cat, and both a skilled hunter and a nimble athlete. It feels at ease anywhere, and is a flexible and accommodating cat with great adaptability.

Japanese Bobtail

The Japanese Bobtail is a supple, agile cat that feels at ease in any situation.

Bi-colored Bobtails are extremely rare. But the absolute pinnacle for all enthusiasts is the Bobtail known as "mi-ke," which has a tri-colored coat: black, white, and red.

The Bobtail, also dubbed the "chrysanthemum cat" because of the shape of its tail, is a poetic and playful animal.

The Bobtail may be practically any color except for lavender, chocolate, or colorpoint.

Although it displays many similarities to the American Shorthair, the British Shorthair is a completely separate breed. It used to be the star of the British cat show scene until the Siamese and Persians usurped its place.

In recent years there has been a spectacular revival of interest in this cat, which is greatly admired even by the most demanding connoisseurs. This old breed became popular toward the end of the nineteenth century, but it was probably originally imported by Roman legionaries who came to Britain almost two thousand years ago after they had colonized Gaul.

The tranquil, accommodating British Shorthair likes to be outdoors, but can easily adapt to an indoor life. It is sweet and affectionate, and always loves to be stroked. This lively, highly intelligent creature is an excellent mouser and a good sprinter. It is crazy about its owner, and makes an ideal pet for children. It gets on extremely well with other cats and, contrary to popular belief, it will also live quite happily with a dog. The kittens are sometimes mischievous and boisterous, but as time goes on they become more calm and mellow. This cat has an insatiable curiosity, and therefore makes an amusing companion.

What is striking is that the coat of the British Shorthair is so woolly—very different from the American Shorthair. Although

British Shorthair

it has no undercoat, its density and elasticity provides protection from the cold and bad weather. The body – thickset, muscular, and stocky, with a broad, deep chest – is large, and is well matched by the broad, powerful head with full cheeks and round eyes. The eyes are often amber in color, but blue and green eyes also occur. It has short, sturdy legs.

The eyes of the British Shorthair are very often orange or copper-colored.

The British Shorthair has a stocky, compact body.

The British Shorthair is perfectly adapted to outdoor living. Indeed, its short, dense coat protects it against bad weather.

The strong, dependable British Shorthair is a cat you can trust completely.

53

The British Shorthair has a very round head with a strong, heavy chin. Its round eyes and small ears are widely spaced.

57

The strong, sturdy body and powerful musculature of the British Shorthair make it seem more compact and more massive than its equivalents, the European Shorthair and the American Shorthair.

The British Shorthair is very protective of its kittens.

Burmilla and Bombay

A cross between a Chinchilla and a Burmese, the Burmilla was born in 1981. The name is a combination of the names of its two parents. It is a lovely, agreeable cat with a lively, sympathetic character.

The Burmilla is an interesting combination of the extroverted Burmese and the imperturbable, tranquil Chinchilla. It is an alluring cat with an elegant, well-proportioned body, and has the most fascinating eyes—exceptionally beautiful, emerald-green rimmed with black, as if with eyeliner. Such large, slanting eyes are not found in any other member of the cat family. Its coat is also striking: silver-white with a characteristic tipping (pigmentation of the tips of the hairs) which may be in any of the colors of the Burmese, from sable to red, via blue, chocolate, lilac, and cream. This is an unassuming, reserved animal (although it does sometimes meow a lot), but it is very fond of the outdoor life and hates to be alone.

The Bombay is another crossbreed in which the Burmese is involved; however, it does not come, as its name would suggest, from India, but from the United States. Nikki Horner, a breeder from Kentucky, wanted a domestic equivalent of the Indian black panther, and achieved this aim by crossing Burmese with black American Shorthairs. It makes a perfect housemate, quite adorable and very reserved, just like the Burmilla. Its meow is very soft and sweet. It is a quiet cat that does not like a lot of commotion. Strangely enough, it does not get on well with other cats. It may, however, strike up friendships with other pets. This playful cat likes its food (it can sometimes be downright greedy), and is extremely intelligent.

The Bombay has gold-colored eyes which stand out against its black coat.

The Bombay's coat, with its very soft, short hair, feels exceptionally silky. It is this handsome, dark coat that makes the breed so costly.

The Bombay is very much a stay-at-home cat, quite happy to spend day after day indoors.

There are few Burmillas in Europe, but the breed is popular in the United States and Canada.

T he Burmese can be amazingly long-lived, often reaching eighteen years of age, and because of its great agility it has remarkable acrobatic talents. It is incredibly cool and courageous, and is one of nature's strong, dominant creatures.

It is extroverted, meows frequently, and loves physical exertion, but never forget that behind the all-powerful facade lies hidden a sensitive—even over-sensitive—cat, which adores its owner, to whom it will become quite exclusively attached. It is a lovely, sociable animal that does not cope well with solitude.

The Burmese breed is divided into two categories. In the European Burmese, a wide range of coat color is permitted (such as red, chocolate, lilac and blue). In the classic American understanding, however, the Burmese is a cat with a dark brown coat, a color known as "sable." This shorthaired cat with the soft, silky coat is medium-sized and quite rounded in shape. A strong, sturdy bone structure and an impressive musculature give an impression of greater than average, and at first sight unexpected, power. Its head is short and triangular, and its ears are rounded at the tips and are widely spaced. Large, round, golden-colored eyes give its face a special sparkle, reflecting the liveliness and intelligence of this cat.

Legend has it that the Burmese is of mythical origin: it is supposed to be a direct descendant of the sacred cats of Burma, divine icons of the Buddhist monasteries.

Burmese

The Burmese has long, thin legs,
while its tail, of medium length,
tapers at the tip.

Dr. Joseph Thompson, a US Navy doctor, brought the first Burmese to the United States from Rangoon, the capital of Burma, in the 1930s. This cat was mated with a Siamese tom.

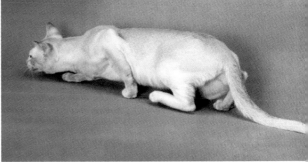

The coat of the Burmese may be blue or even lilac in color, but also cream, chocolate, or red.

The Burmese is a very affectionate breed and the females are loving mothers to their kittens.

With its very short, very silky coat, the Burmese looks as shiny as satin.

The Burmese has a short nose and high cheekbones. Its ears have slightly rounded tips.

I n 1558 the French poet Joachim du Bellay praised his Chartreux, named Belaud, which he loved with a passion, as the most beautiful work that nature has ever wrought in the way of cats.

The Chartreux, an old friend in literary circles, was also the favorite cat of Colette, who was mad about cats. ("Will I ever be crazy enough about animals?" she once asked.) This cat was the inspiration for her novel *La Chatte*. She called him her "little bear with chubby cheeks," her "blue dove," her "pearl-colored demon." Charles de Gaulle's best friend was a Chartreux called Ringo de Balmalon. His wife Yvonne found this name rather a mouthful, and gave him the simpler name Gris-Gris. Gris-Gris was witness to the endless games of solitaire that the General used to play toward the end of his life in the quiet seclusion of Colombey. Although the Chartreux is sometimes confused with the British Blue, it is most definitely a French cat, par excellence. There is a legend that the monks who invented the famous Chartreuse liqueur brought the cat with them from Africa and developed the breed in their monastery. What is more likely is that the name comes from a soft, silky, gray wool called "pile des chartreux."

It is very beautiful and very elegant, and its doll-like head, which is a good match for its muscular body, is shaped like an upside-down trapezoid. It harbors a deep affection for its owner, whom it will happily accompany on long walks in the outdoors. If its owner is far away, it is quite capable of starving itself to death. But this matchless hunter with a healthy appetite is seldom sick. The

Chartreux

Chartreux is much sought after among cat-lovers, and is therefore well worth the price to be paid because of its rarity. It is virtually a cult cat, a status of course due in part to its prestigious owners, but more than that to its pleasing character: it is a quiet and loyal companion with an unparalleled aura of poetry.

The Chartreux has been the favorite cat of countless famous people.

91

The Chartreux has beautiful amber eyes.

The Chartreux was the favorite cat of Colette, though she idolized innumerable breeds of cat.

The Chartreux is a very unusual cat that evokes thoughts of luxury and prestige.

With its doll-like face, the Chartreux looks like a soft, cuddly toy.

T he Bengal, a striking crossbreed, is the result of a specific scientific experiment: research into natural resistance to leukosis in the Leopard Cats of Southeast Asia.

The Bengal is the product of one of these Asian Leopard Cats and an American Shorthair; the crossbreeding took place in the United States at the beginning of the 1970s. The breeding program focused on producing a miniature "leopard" with the adaptable, friendly nature of the best of house cats.

Its coat is spotted, just like a leopard's,

Bengal

while its legs are striped and its tail, dark at the tip, is ringed. These different markings may be cinnamon, black, or chocolate. The background color of its coat is either a clear, rich red, almost orange, or else white (in the case of the variant known as the "Snow Bengal"). A golden sheen accentuates the extraordinary beauty of this thick, silky coat. The Bengal has a large, powerful, muscular body. Its triangular head can, however, seem a little small in relation to its body. Its ears are widely spaced, with rounded tips, and its eyes may be any color, though they are most often green. The tail tends to be carried rather low.

From its wild origins, it has retained its love of outdoor adventure. It is an energetic garden cat that needs to be in touch with nature. This outstanding hunter loves to be active and comes fully into its own only in the outdoors. It must not be shut up indoors for too long or it will waste away. Its wild-cat looks, even in its miniature form, can be disconcerting, even frightening. In fact, however, the Bengal is as gentle as a lamb. The rare outbursts of aggression it sometimes displays are never dangerous. It loves to have children around.

Contrary to its appearance, the Bengal is an exceptionally gentle, loving cat.

The bright, warm personality of the Bengal will bring an exotic, fanciful touch into the home.

The Bengal sometimes seems to behave like a wild animal, and may have a slightly aggressive attitude, but it is never dangerous—in fact quite the opposite.

The Bengal usually has green eyes, and its head is generally longer than it is wide.

Few cats are the subject of so
many myths and legends as
the Manx.

I t is quite common for a legend to be associated with the origins of a breed of cat. The magical powers readily attributed to these animals go right back to the beginning of their history, and tales of adventure and mythology are substituted for the scientific reality.

The Manx cat, from the Isle of Man, attracts perhaps the largest number of tales of this kind, no doubt because of an essential morphological peculiarity: it has no tail. This makes it a unique cat, although in the cat world there are plenty of special cases and remark-

Manx

able exceptions. Thus, it is said that the Manx cat's tail was caught in the doors of the Ark when Noah closed them, and that the amputated tail was washed away by the raging Flood. Or else, again in the Ark, that a wicked dog bit it off. It is also said that the barbarian warriors of the Isle of Man were in the habit of cutting off the tails of their cats when they won a battle to decorate the rims of their shining helmets. Another story claims that the breed developed from cats on board a Spanish ship that ran aground between Ireland and England in the sixteenth century. But so much for the stories. The truth is no doubt very different, but remains unclear. The Manx cat is certainly no rare beauty; it is often likened to a rabbit, with which it shares the same gait and agility. Its coat is thick, and all colors are permitted, from solid to bi-colored to tabby. The Manx, a devoted and loving cat, is intelligent and docile, and likes to be active. The home-loving Manx makes an ideal companion for the whole family, and is a textbook indoor cat.

The head of the Manx cat is broad and round. Its neck is short and powerful, and its wide-spaced ears are slightly rounded at the tip.

Although the Manx is not exactly a beautiful cat, it does seem to make an excellent pet, totally devoted and very loving.

The Mau, whose name means both "cat" and "light" in Egyptian, is undoubtedly the patriarch of all the domestic cats of the world. Images of this companion, emblem of the pharaohs, can be seen in tombs and on papyrus scrolls from as early as 1500 BC. It was not just an animal, but the sacred symbol of an entire people. Even the sun-god Ra was sometimes depicted as a Mau.

The Mau, the only naturally spotted breed of cat, is an incomparable beauty. Its fine, supple coat is silky smooth and glossy. It has striped legs and comes in three colors: silver, bronze, and smoke. The contrast between the spots and the background color is very marked, which is why it is often likened to a small domestic leopard. A powerful musculature, supported by a strong skeleton, sets off its perfectly proportioned body superbly. It is elegant without being thin, sturdy without being bulky. The eyes of the most striking specimens are of an intense pale green known

Egyptian Mau

In the 1950s an exiled Russian princess, Natalia Troubetzkoy, living in exile in the United States, brought a number of these cats out of Egypt, via Italy. She began breeding Maus, which, owing to their rarity, have since become hugely desirable among all kinds of collectors. But strangely enough, despite having been in existence for centuries, the Mau only received recognition as a breed in the 1970s.

as "gooseberry green." The Mau's long legs make it an outstanding sprinter, one of the fastest cats there is. When it is trotting, it looks as if it is running on tiptoe.

The Mau is very selective in its attachments, but once it has accepted its owner, it is a congenial, docile, quiet cat. It does not like to be alone, and gets along very well with other cats.

The Mau is very sociable and affectionate, and brings tenderness and simplicity to the home.

Despite the almost god-like aura attributed to the Mau, it is more fragile than it looks. It needs constant care and attention.

The Mau has an "M" on its forehead, extending over its head and neck.

The Mau is an athletic cat that likes exercise now and again, but it does not have a boisterous temperament, and adapts perfectly well to indoor living.

The European Shorthair is one of the oldest breeds of cat in the world. Traces of it can be found in documents as far back as the ninth century. Although it is often wrongly confused with the alley cat, it is truly purebred – despite its natural origins and its unremarkable form – and as a result of which it really does, look like the archetypal domestic cat.

For this reason it took a long time for the breed to be recognized (1983), and among purists it was for a long time the most controversial of cats. Its looks are certainly not unappealing, but it lacks the originality of specific traits or features, whether aesthetic or unusual, that would make it striking. It is also often confused with the British Shorthair and the American Shorthair. This is not surprising, since they are its direct descendants, but they are simply more elegant and graceful. Its body is thickset and sturdy, and of medium size. Its slightly rounded head is supported by a muscular neck. Its erect, widely spaced ears are held above a somewhat domed forehead. Its tail is not long and its legs are very strong. Its short, shiny coat may be any color except lilac, chocolate, or colorpoint. Its large, oblique eyes go well with the color of its coat.

Although the European Shorthair cannot boast any great morphological virtues, it nevertheless has a certain charm: the charm of the familiar. It is this familiarity that gives the breed its magic. It is, so to speak, the quintessential cat, the most obvious representative of its race; a reassuring, reliable housemate that we feel we have known forever.

European Shorthair

The European Shorthair is an exceptionally quiet, affectionate animal, radiating feelings of ease and reassurance.

Unlike the alley cat, the European Shorthair is a true purebred.

The European Shorthair is of a well-balanced build. Its slightly rounded face, its pronounced nose and its round, somewhat slanting eyes give a sense of peace and simplicity.

The gaze of the Exotic
Shorthair is particularly
intense and endearing.

The Exotic Shorthair combines the serenity of the Persian with the independence of the American Shorthair. This is not surprising, since it was created from the union of these two breeds. In the 1950s, breeders were trying to produce a cat similar to the Persian, but with shorter fur, partly to make the animal easier to care for.

The cross was a total success with a stunning result. The coat of the Exotic, which is longer than that of the other Shorthairs, is gorgeous, dense, silky, and extremely plush. Short, stocky legs support a thickset, compact body, an imposing head with full cheeks and an incredibly straight, short tail. These physical characteristics are largely responsible for the quiet strength and imperturbability, that these cats seem always to emanate.

The calm, sweet-natured Exotic Shorthair is a docile, easy-going cat, not very noisy (hardly ever meowing), with an exceptionally agreeable, friendly nature and of exemplary discretion. Furthermore, it is not at all difficult to care for. It is a well-balanced cat, very adaptable, which loves plenty of space and the outdoors, where it can give free rein to its hunting instincts. But it will also happily tolerate a life indoors, which makes it the perfect cat for apartment-dwellers. It is an ideal cat for children, who adore its teddy-bear looks; it gets along extremely well with them, displaying its affectionate, playful side without reserve, and it is unusually tolerant. The overall impression of roundness and good humor, of mild-

Exotic Shorthair

mannered pride, make this "Persian in pajamas" the epitome of the family cat.

The Exotic Shorthair has an especially large head. With its fat, full cheeks and its thick, muscular neck, it looks like a cuddly toy.

The fur of the Exotic Shorthair is longer than that of the British Shorthair or the American Shorthair.

Although it has all the characteristics of the Persian, the Exotic Shorthair is classed as a shorthaired cat.

The Exotic Shorthair enjoys life, loves eating, and embodies roundness and softness.

151

The alley cat naturally defies
the classifications of pedigree
cats.

Alley Cat

The alley cat, that familiar, popular, folksy animal, does not belong to any particular breed, and cannot be said to have a pedigree. It comes from everywhere and nowhere, it is both independent and affectionate—and that is why we love it.

There have, of course, been attempts to categorize it, and give it an artificial identity, a standard. It should have short fur, green eyes, a round head . . . But the alley cat, or "house cat," is like a chameleon and it can take on any shape: shorthaired, semi-longhaired, or longhaired; coats of various colors; eyes blue, green, chestnut . . . It is accommodating and adaptable, and no other cat can satisfy in quite the same way the fantasy image of its owner, who ultimately is the only person who can say whether the animal meets his or her desires. If you take in an alley cat, you should be prepared for a few surprises. The fact that there are so many of them, and that the price is ridiculously low compared with that of a pedigree cat, brings in an element of uncertainty, and the owner therefore takes a gamble on the true temperament of the animal. There are owners who have torn their hair out in despair when the terrible truth has dawned on them: the delicate little creature, the little treasure, that they fell for has turned out to be a capricious demon, a freeloader, and very noisy! We know the character of the Tonkinese, of the Maine Coon, and of the Siamese (sometimes atrocious!). But we don't know the character of a stray, whose origin is unknown. However, the temperament of the ideal alley cat—of which there are, in fact, many—is much better than its appearance would sometimes suggest.

The alley cat habitually roams the streets and the countryside, alone or in a group.

If an alley cat is taken into the home and becomes accustomed to people, it seems to make an amenable and sensitive companion.

The alley cat is the textbook sociable cat which likes both children and other cats.

Shorthaired Cats

The independent and, at the same time, affectionate temperament of the alley cat makes it one of the loveliest cats.

With so many different kinds of alley cat, coat, size, and build are very variable. There is no standard.

167

The simple, often sensitive alley cat might be regarded as the ideal kind of cat.

T he oldest traces that have been found of the Korat date from the sixteenth century in the Thai manuscript *Tamra Meow*, in which there is a cat called Si Sah-Waht whose description matches completely what some people still call the "Blue Siamese."

The Korat, which is still rare even now, does in fact have a beautiful blue coat with silver - tipped hairs. This cat, which is longer-lived than average (the Korat can reach the age of thirty), is considered to be the most intelligent cat there is.

In 1974 Hal and Tommy Meadows, an American couple on vacation in Singapore, were the first Westerners to take an interest in the Singapura, a feral cat found on the streets of the island. Back in the United States, Tommy and Hal soon showed the cat, and they achieved great success. Although the Singapura is very small, as a well-proportioned cat, it makes a very different impression from the Munchkin. Because of its adaptability, this quiet, well-balanced cat will cope anywhere, and it makes a lovely, affectionate companion. It is a very good house cat.

The Munchkin owes its strange name to Victor Fleming's film The Wizard of Oz. It was the name of the diminutive people that the young Dorothy met during her wanderings through the imaginary land of Oz. It is sometimes also called the "basset cat" or the "dachshund cat" because it has very short legs, which give it the gait of a very young cat. This peculiarity is the result of a natural mutation, and it was only discovered recently, in the 1990s, in the United States.

Korat, Singapura, and Munchkin

The Singapura may be known in its country of origin as the "sewer cat," but the Singapura is one of the most expensive and sought-after pedigree cats.

The eyes of the Korat are usually green. Its playful, energetic nature makes it a highly valued companion.

Its "dwarf" cat status makes the Munchkin
tremendously endearing.

The sweet, sensitive Munchkin
has an ideal personality.

The Oriental Shorthair has
unforgettable almond-shaped,
emerald or jade green eyes.

The Oriental Shorthair is in a sense the sibling of the Siamese, and some even claim that it is the ancestor of the Siamese. In the nineteenth century, British diplomats, who were influenced by the exoticism and mystery of the country, brought back from Thailand a number of these cats that so resemble the Siamese. (Only the coat differs, being of solid color).

But at the beginning of the twentieth century, the colossal success of the true Siamese completely wrecked the "career" of the Oriental Shorthair. It was not until the 1960s that a breeder named Pat Turner developed a comparable breed. She crossed the Siamese with the American Shorthair, the British Shorthair and the European Shorthair in an attempt to produce a white Siamese. A modern version of the Oriental Shorthair was born. The Oriental Shorthair, an elegant cat with a strong, steely personality, though it is much easier to live with and much more sweet-natured than the Siamese, now has a reputation all of its own. It is greatly prized by a large band of fervent admirers all over the world.

In the 1950s the British Baroness von Ullman produced a Havana Brown (or Chestnut Havana) by crossing a chocolate Siamese with a black European Shorthair. It was later named simply the Havana, in

Oriental Shorthair and Havana Brown

honor of the famous cigar, or, according to some, after a breed of rabbit of the same color, a very specific shade of mahogany.

The tall, slender Oriental Shorthair evokes harmony and light.

The Oriental Shorthair, which is related to the Siamese, is much better-natured than its "sibling."

The rather muscular Oriental
Shorthair has a short, very
dense coat.

The head of the Oriental Shorthair, with its straight profile and narrow jaw, has the striking shape of an equilateral triangle.

191

The Oriental Shorthair is highly sensitive, a trait which makes it very endearing to its owner.

The Oriental Shorthair forms an exclusive attachment to the person who cares for it, becoming virtually bonded to that person.

The Havana Brown is slim
and elegant, has a long body,
and is very strong. Its forelegs
are shorter than its hind legs,
and it has a very beautiful,
long, thin tail.

197

I n 1950, **Kallibunker was born on Bodmin Moor in Cornwall; it was a cat with curly hair, the result of a spontaneous mutation in a litter of kittens, the rest of which all looked normal. A new breed was developed, the Cornish Rex, all descended from Kallibunker.**

Exactly ten years later, another cat with a curly coat saw the light of day: Kirlee, the product of a cross between two feral cats. Breeders mated the cat with a Cornish Rex, but this produced kittens with normal coats, without any curls. And so the Cornish Rex and the Devon Rex developed as separate breeds.

In 1987 another curly cat appeared, this time in the United States, near the Selkirk Mountains in the heart of Wyoming. This was crossed with a black Persian, and from this mating the progeny of the Selkirk Rex were able to spread.

Whatever the breed, the Rexes have a strong, well-developed musculature. The Selkirk Rex is undoubtedly the most robust of the three. The Cornish and the Devon have a finer, very lean and elegant body. The curly or wavy coat of the Rexes is short, especially in the Cornish, and very soft. The coat of the Devon is stiffer. The Selkirk takes ten months to grow its adult coat, but all coat colors and patterns are possible.

Every owner says: there are few cats as sweet-natured and gentle as the Rexes. Their overwhelming affection seems inexhaustible. They are unflappable, their self-

Cornish, Devon and Selkirk Rex

possession is majestic, and they are strongly attached to home and family.

The Selkirk Rex is a Rex of American origin, not yet recognized by the official bodies.

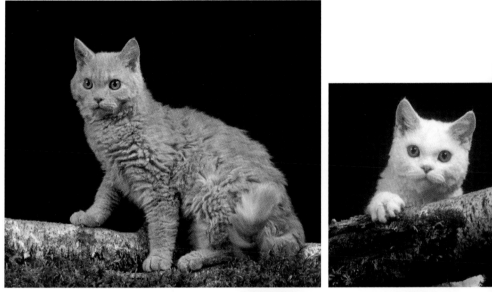

Nicknamed the "cat in sheep's clothing," the Selkirk Rex is more muscular, with a stronger skeletal structure than the other Rexes.

With its long, thin, muscular legs,
the Devon Rex is a good acrobat.

Like all the Rexes, the Devon Rex is very agile and athletic, so it is a good sprinter and can jump high and far.

The Devon Rex is a sensitive, genuine cat much loved by children.

The Rexes always have wedge-shaped heads with prominent cheekbones. The skull is flat and the neck long and thin.

The Cornish Rex was the first of the Rexes.

211

The Rexes do not require much maintenance, but they have a bigger appetite than other cats. This is due to their faster metabolism and their higher body temperature. They therefore need a lot of food.

Whereas the ears of the American Curl form a crescent shape, those of the Scottish Fold are actually folded flat against its skull. It is often said that the Scottish Fold comes from China; tales of sightings of cats with flattened ears were regularly brought back from Asia in the nineteenth century.

In fact, as its name suggests, this cat comes from Perthsire, Scotland. In 1961 a man called William Ross, who was crossbreeding American and British Shorthairs, spotted a kitten with malformed ears and began developing a new breed from this cat. The Scottish Fold has been very successful in the United States. However, because of its rather brittle bones, caused by the same gene responsible for the ear mutation, it is not officially recognized in all countries.

At birth, the Scottish Fold has erect ears that fold over after three weeks. If the ears stay upright, the kitten is a Scottish Straight, which, according to some people, is the same as a British Shorthair. There is also a longhaired version of the Scottish Fold, called the Highland Fold.

The Scottish Fold will always have a very remarkable personality all of its own, accentuated by the shape of its ears: a thoroughly characteristic mixture of friendliness and melancholy that makes it undeniably beautiful and compelling. Its nature, well matched to its physique, is extremely sweet and sensitive. It is a treasure of a cat, and children are more aware of that than anyone. It is choosy about whom it

Scottish Fold

becomes attached to. Once it has made its choice, it will show that person a deep and exclusive love.

The Scottish Fold has a rather odd shape: a strong, stocky body on quite short legs.

The tail of the Scottish Fold is full and very thick at its base, and is never longer than two-thirds of the length of its body.

The Scottish Fold is an endearing cat, overflowing with love and tenderness.

Everything about the shape of
the Siamese, from its legs to
its neck and tail, gives the
impression of grace and
suppleness.

T he Siamese is a star, the mythical cat par excellence. Its mysterious and splendid origins have lent it the status of a sacrosanct icon. The ancestry of this ancient breed will never be known.

The first mention of it is found in a manuscript from the fourteenth century from the then capital of Siam, Ayuthia. From this we know that it was a sacred animal, the subject of immense veneration. But the main thing we know is that this probable descendant of the Asian wild cat was the favorite (and only) companion of the kings of Siam. At the end of the nineteenth

Siamese

century, a British diplomat was given two Siamese cats by the King of Siam. He immediately showed them in his home country, where they caused great excitement, eventually resulting in the dissemination of the breed throughout Europe and the United States.

Certainly it seems perfectly apt to talk of "aristocratic elegance" when describing this cat, which lived in the closed circles of the temples and the most luxurious chambers of the Orient, and to refer to it as the "prince among cats."

The Siamese is not a placid animal. It is well known for its absolutist and extreme personality. Even the most indulgent owner will not be spared its caprices. It is restless and rambunctious, and is noted for its yowling and meowing. There are few cats so changeable in mood, so unpredictable in nature, and so bewildering. Nevertheless, in spite of all these daunting faults, it is difficult not to love this exceptionally intelligent and sensitive creature. Its sometimes aggressive facade conceals a heart of gold, and at times it can be immoderately delightful. In fact, "immoderate" is the adjective that probably best describes this extraordinary cat.

Exquisite, almond-shaped, piercingly bright blue eyes beam out of the triangular head of the Siamese, with its pointed, wide-spaced ears.

With its exclusive temperament, the Siamese demands constant attention and commitment.

227

The excessively egocentric personality of the Siamese makes it sometimes difficult to live with.

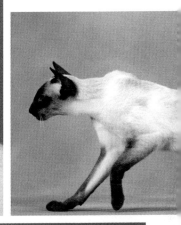

The Siamese is a seductive cat that is difficult to resist.

T he Sphynx, a bizarre cat that some find repulsive and others fascinating, has an exceptionally sweet, gentle personality, even though its appearance might suggest otherwise.

This remarkable animal probably originated in Aztec Mexico, where it was revered. References to it are found at the beginning of the twentieth century and later, in about 1935. But it was not until the mid-1960s that this cat began to be bred in Ontario, Canada. As a result of a natural mutation, the Sphynx, often dubbed the "naked cat," has skin covered with only a light, barely visible down, with wrinkles on the neck and legs. This gives it a soft, silky feel.

Because of its lack of fur, it has to stay indoors, as it cannot tolerate extremes of temperature. It requires careful, meticulous, and frequent maintenance, because the nakedness of its skin means there is no hair to absorb perspiration and it can become rather oily and dirty. In the winter it requires more food in order to withstand the cold. It will eat both canned food and fresh food, and it likes vegetables. The kittens of the Sphynx are very fragile, and many of them die. For this reason, the breed is rare.

The Ocicat is so called because as a kitten it looks like an ocelot, a wild cat from Central and Southern America. That, at any rate, was what the daughter of the breeder thought when she gave it its name. In 1964 in Berkeley, Michigan, Virginia Daly crossed

Sphynx and Ocicat

a Siamese with an Abyssinian, in the hopes of obtaining a Siamese with Abyssinian-type points. This animal was subsequently crossed with an American Shorthair. The result, the Ocicat, with the golden-brown, spotted coat of a wild cat, was not recognized until much later, in the mid-1980s.

The Sphynx, very playful but sometimes a bit wild, frightened of other cats but possessive toward its owner, has a home-loving temperament.

The docile, friendly Ocicat is a loner that does not much care for the company of other cats. Because of its solitary behavior, it almost seems like a wild animal.

The Tonkinese is a sweet,
lively cat, far less aloof than
its cousin, the Siamese.

Like the Bombay, the Tonkinese is a hybrid breed, the successful result of an experiment by breeders looking for something new. It arose from a cross between two cats from Asia, the Burmese and the Siamese.

The "Tonk," as it is sometimes known, is a handsome mix of its two parents. However, although it has the beautiful coat of the Burmese, in general it inherits much more from the Siamese: its head, slenderness, legs, and tail. The elegant body of the Tonkinese is strong and impressively muscled. Its thin tail is of medium length and its hind legs are longer than its forelegs. It carries a triangular head on a neck of medium length. It has a square jaw (slightly more so than the Siamese) and widely spaced ears. Otherwise, the Tonkinese owes much of its reputation to its eyes, which are a bright, piercing blue-green.

The Tonkinese, which can be a rather lively cat, thrives better out of doors, especially if there are trees it can climb. Provided it is properly trained, however, it can also make a docile, careful house cat. It is lively, inquisitive, and full of an irresistible energy; it adores playing, and children are its favorite companions.

The Pixie Bob, another rather unusual hybrid cat, is supposed to be descended from the bobcat. That, at any rate, was what the owner of the first Pixie Bob claimed, and

Tonkinese and Pixie Bob

it does indeed look very much like a wild cat. Its character, however, is sweet and gentle, and it is the ideal domestic cat, very attached to its owner.

The Tonkinese, a well-muscled but refined animal of medium build, is the perfect cross between a Siamese and a Burmese.

The wild nature of the Pixie Bob is just an illusion: it has no love of solitude and enjoys being indoors.

251

The Pixie Bob, which physically looks like a wild cat (some claim that it is descended from the bobcat), is in fact an exemplary house cat, never aggressive or unsociable. It is playful, and mixes very well with other cats.

Semi-long-haired Cats

The lovely, energetic Turkish Van is not much of a house cat. It will always prefer a garden to an apartment, a lake shore to a balcony. It is an adventurer, an athlete and loves running and climbing trees. But, above, all it loves swimming, which earns it not only the nickname of the "Turkish Swimming Cat," but also a unique status among cats. The Turkish Van has a soft, supple, long or semi-long coat which protects it superbly well against the cold, despite having no woolly undercoat. It is a uniform white color.

The origins of the Turkish Van lie far in the past. It was first seen in Turkey, in the snowy regions around Lake Van. Having been taken to the United Kingdom by breeder Laura Lushington in 1955, the breed was recognized there in 1970, and was recognized for Championship status in the United States in 1994.

The Turkish Angora comes from Anatolia Turkey, and takes its name from Ankara, the Turkish capital, which used to be called Angora. After nearly disapeearing as a breed for several centuries, it was eventually rediscovered after the Second World War and in the 1950s was introduced to the United States, where it has been very successful. It is a very elegant cat, majestic and graceful, with a silky, shining coat and long,

Turkish Van and Turkish Angora

pointed ears. Its enigmatic air and the motionless pose it sometimes adopts invite comparisons with the sphinx from Greek mythology. This intelligent and playful animal, with its exceptionally lively spirit, a rival of the Persian, is extremely beautiful and much in demand.

The Turkish Angora requires less grooming than the Persian, because its undercoat is not very long.

261

The Turkish Angora, which was once very fashionable in the French Court, is quite a slender, graceful animal.

The Turkish Angora has a rather narrow, triangular head with a pretty pink nose and erect, pointed ears.

The coat of the Turkish Angora can vary in color, but white is the most desirable.

There are few Turkish Vans in Europe, despite the fact that the breed was developed in the United Kingdom.

Its even white coat may have brown or auburn patches on the head, the ears, and even all along the hindquarters down to the tail.

The forelegs of the Turkish Van are shorter than its hind legs, and it has characteristic tufts of hair between its paws.

Despite its name, the Balinese is purely the product of American breeding. It owes its name to the impression of grace it invokes, reminiscent of the suppleness and lightness of the dancers of the Indonesian island of Bali.

Two breeders from California, Marion Dorset and Helen Smith, were the first to begin developing this breed in the 1940s; over the following ten years its numbers increased greatly.

Balinese

The cats did not appear in Europe until later, in the 1970s.

The Balinese is the result of a mutation in the Siamese, and for that reason was for a long time not regarded very highly. Its nickname is the "longhaired Siamese." It is a very beautiful cat, with its silky, ermine-like coat flowing flat against its body. It is supple and slender, and stands on long legs. Its triangular head has large, pointed ears that are very often tufted. It has lovely, almond-shaped blue eyes. The kittens are white to begin with, only acquiring their definitive color after a year. The four main colors for the points are the same as for the Siamese: seal, blue, chocolate, and lilac. In the United States, Balinese that do not have these colors are called Javanese. In Europe, no such distinction is made.

The personality of the Balinese is generally the same as that of the pure pedigree Siamese. Just like the Siamese, it is a born athlete, an incredible acrobat that can execute the most precarious leaps with alarming ease. Furthermore, the Balinese is also sexually very active, and needs plenty of space and open air to blossom to the full. It is an extrovert that knows exactly what it wants and is quite capable of letting you know by means of loud meows and an array of expressive postures.

The Balinese is a very seductive cat that will not hesitate to use its charm to get what it wants.

The Balinese does not like solitude, and therefore prefers to live in a group.

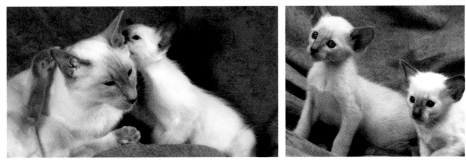

This cat, dubbed the "long-haired Siamese," has a coat with colored points.

Because it is rather uncertain where this breed comes from, a number of myths have arisen, one of the most bizarre being that it is descended from the raccoon. Although there is a certain similarity between the two, this yarn seems, from a genetic point of view, to be highly unlikely. Nonetheless, it is noteworthy that the Maine owes half its name to the word "coon," an abbreviation for "raccoon."

in Maine, and it may possibly be the oldest breed in America. It was, incidentally, only recognized as a breed in its homeland in 1967.

It is one of the most admired cats in the whole world. The greatest aesthetes among cat-lovers hold it up as a model because of its perfection of form. Its impressive frame is one of the main reasons for its prestigious reputation. A full-grown Maine Coon is large, muscular, and strong, and can sometimes weigh nearly 20 pounds. Because of its unusually thick double coat, it delights people who like to stroke cats: they go crazy over its long, silky fur. Its legs are thick and sturdy. Its long tail is thin, but shaggy. Its round head has a square jaw

Maine Coon

The most likely explanation of its origin comes, unsurprisingly, from the state of Maine, in the nineteenth century. It is thought that the breed came about as a result of crossbreeding between indigenous cats and longhaired Angoras. It was at that time the favorite cat of the big farmers

and beautiful ears set wide apart, ending in tufts called "lynx tips." Its eyes may be any color, and likewise its coat, except for lilac, cinnamon, fawn, chocolate, or colorpoint. The Maine Coon is particularly affectionate, and is sensitive and gentle with children.

The head of the Maine Coon looks small compared to its body. Its large ears are adorned with tufts.

285

The Maine Coon is a particularly friendly and loving cat.

The Maine Coon is the most popular cat in the United States, although it has competition from the Persian.

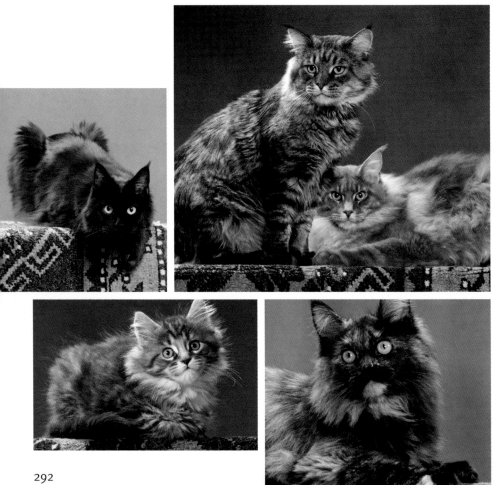

According to one legend, the Maine Coon is descended from one of Marie Antoinette's favorite cats.

There are no precise rules as to the color of the eyes or coat of the Maine Coon.

If well-trained, the Maine Coon can make an excellent house cat.

Maine Coon kittens grow relatively slowly. They only reach their full adult size after about four years.

The Maine Coon has a round
face with a strong chin
and a square jaw.

The bright blue, oval eyes of
the Ragdoll are incredibly
beautiful.

A strange creature, the Ragdoll! It is said to feel no pain and to perceive no danger. This is not true, of course, but is what some people believe because of its very curious and atypical behavior.

The fact is that this aptly named cat forms its relationships with others (its owner, other cats) through absolute submission, which some regard as spineless. It seems it cannot (or can no longer) defend itself, and its aggression is buried as deep as it could possibly be. If it is picked up or stroked it immediately goes limp, never showing any sign that it might feel like putting out its claws—it could never be so unfriendly, it seems. Some attribute this behavior to weak muscle tone. Others, who take more of a psychoanalytical approach, go further and talk about an underlying incident, an original trauma that is supposed to have determined the personality of the entire breed: a road accident suffered by the mother of the very first Ragdolls. Whatever may be the case, this cat seems to make an adorable pet. The Ragdoll has Olympian reserves of calmness, and wears its heart on its sleeve: it shows its indolent friendliness by sweetly and meekly following its owner everywhere. You could not wish for a more stable, well-balanced cat. It is, of course, no outstanding hunter or athlete, but its lively spirit does make it an extremely agreeable playmate. This cat of recent American origin (first bred in the 1960s in Riverside, California) is a beautiful half-breed: half Persian, half Birman. Its lovely, silky-smooth, semi-long coat does not develop until adulthood. Ragdolls are impressive in terms of their size and weight, and are very powerful-looking.

Ragdoll

The coat of the Ragdoll is usually bicolored, although a variety of colors is permitted.

305

The Ragdoll has very widely-spaced ears with quite rounded tips, which point slightly forward.

The Sacred Birman is often regarded as the classic example of calmness and balance, but it is certainly no doormat, no hesitant, timid, complaisant creature that submits to the demands of its owner. On the contrary, it has an impressively strong personality. It is playful, mischievous, and intelligent. This excellent indoor cat knows how to charm the whole family and brings wisdom and tranquility to the home.

With its large, deep blue, almost perfectly round eyes, it is enormously seductive. The origins of the Sacred Birman are rather vague, but collective memory prefers legend, often better remembered if it is more entrancing than the truth. The story goes that in a Buddhist temple in Burma there once lived many cats. One of these cats watched over a priest, his master. One day, the priest was killed by bandits and, in despair, the cat called on the goddess of the temple for help. The eyes of the cat turned sapphire-blue like those of the goddess, and its paws turned as white

Sacred Birman

For a long time it was not popular, but it is now one of the most highly valued cats in the world. The most striking feature of the Birman is its "gloved" paws: its paws do indeed have symmetrical white markings that make it look as if its feet are encased in little white ankle-boots! This cat's entire shape seems to be a precise reflection of its character: harmony and proportion, hand–in hand with elegance.

as the hair of the monk. And thereupon all the temple cats underwent the same transformation.

The Sacred Birman has a steely, strong-willed character.

313

The Birman has an exclusive, and some would say passionate, attachment to its owner.

The silky coat of the Birman forms a luxuriant collar framing its face.

319

The history of the Birman is cloaked in magic and mystery.

Of all cats, the Norwegian
Forest Cat is perhaps the
closest to nature.

The Norwegian Forest Cat, this wild feline with a touch of magic, this "enchanted cat," protagonist in countless Scandinavian traditional tales, was, according to mythology, the emblem and companion of Freya, goddess of love and fertility.

It was supposed to have been brought back from Asia by the Vikings in the ninth century. First living in the pine forests of Norway, at the beginning of the twentieth century it was domesticated, after which it became a reliable pet. It was first shown in 1938, but not until the end of the 1970s was it recognized by the International Cat Association.

The sometimes extreme climate of its country of origin has made the Norwegian Forest Cat very resilient. Its semi-long double coat, which makes it look a bit like the Maine Coon, provides protection against severe cold, as does the fur on its tail and ears. Its large, long, muscular body is supported on particularly strong legs. Its triangular head appears round because it has a fringe of long hairs. Its eyes are almond-shaped, and can be all colors, and similarly its coat can vary enormously in color and pattern. Although the Norwegian Forest Cat can now adapt to human rules, it will always remain independent. Because it has always had contact with the forces of nature, it makes a pitiful indoor cat. If it is shut up for any length of time it becomes distressed and wastes away. The outdoors is its domain, and freedom, its true kingdom. To thrive, it needs the space to live life to the fullest, and that is what it chiefly does. This great adventurer is an exceptionally good hunter, and the fearlessness it needs for this derives from its robustness as a natural athlete.

Norwegian Forest Cat

The thick, heavy winter coat of the Norwegian Forest Cat protects it from the cold and rain.

The Norwegian Forest Cat, although it does not respond well to authority and is reserved toward people, can be sweet and affectionate toward its owner, provided it is always given enough free play.

The Norwegian Forest Cat is infinitely tolerant toward other cats. It prefers to live in a group, and does not like being alone.

There is something in the demeanor and mentality of the Norwegian Forest Cat that is reminiscent of the lynx.

It is best not to try to curb the impulses of a creature so sure of its needs and desires.

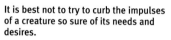

The coat of the Norwegian Forest Cat may be any color except for chocolate, lilac, and colorpoint.

337

The Somali breed was developed in America in the 1960s by Evelyn Mague, and is a sort of long-haired Abyssinian. Kittens like this sometimes occurring in litters of Abyssinians as a result of genetic mutation were initially regarded as abnormal, and were therefore not recognized, but later the breeding of these "Somalis" was encouraged.

The Somali was recognized in the United States only in the 1970s. It has a magnificent, thick coat with ticking that reflects the light beautifully, its demeanor is both aristocratic and at the same time timid, and it is larger than the Abyssinian. Its wonderfully soft, semi-long coat gives it a very particular beauty. It has a minimum of three bands of color on each hair, and some animals have as many as ten. Its fur lies flat along its spine. Its long

Somali

body and thin legs, ending in oval paws, give this much-admired cat an uncommon elegance. Its large, pointed ears are strikingly tufted. Its long, bushy tail is what gives it its nickname "fox cat," or sometimes even "squirrel cat." From its rounded but still triangular head protrudes a delightful, elongated jaw. Its coat can be a variety of colors, but there are four main types: ruddy, which is practically golden-brown; red or sorrel—a rich red; blue; and a creamy-colored fawn. Its almond-shaped eyes may be amber, green or hazel.

This athletic, agile, nervous and intelligent cat needs a lot of space, and will not tolerate being confined for long periods.

The Somali loves nature and freedom. It is a superb, tenacious hunter.

The Somali adores playing, and will happily play with its owner, with whom it forms a permanent bond.

The Somali is calmer and more restful than the Abyssinian, with which it may sometimes interbreed.

Despite its apparently cautious nature, the Somali is sometimes prone to odd changes of mood, making it sometimes a bit excitable and noisy.

Strange as it may seen, given its very recent recognition, the Siberian cat is centuries old.

The first references to it go back more than a thousand years in the north of Russia and in the area around St. Petersburg. Many claim that it is the ancestor of all the long-haired pedigree breeds and the descendant of the European domestic cat, which it very much resembles. It is sometimes called the Siberian Forest Cat, or the Siberian, or even the Sib or Sibi.

The Siberian Cat is quite similar to the Norwegian Forest Cat and the Maine Coon, being a large cat with a powerful body. Everything about this

Siberian Cat

cat is round and sturdy: its broad chest, arched back, long legs, trapezoid-shaped head. It radiates an aura of impressive power spectacular for a cat. Its thick coat is silky-soft. Its tail is long, and tapers to a point. Its eyes are large and almost round and may be any color, irrespective of coat color. Its ears are more rounded than pointed, widely spaced, hairy on the insides and tufted (with lynx tips). There is also a

Siberian colorpoint with blue eyes, called Neva Masquerade.

The Siberian Cat is an exemplary, remarkably tranquil cat, which, despite its independent nature, will happily accept the comfortable life of a house cat. Provided it is able to hunt and climb, it will show itself to be an adorable, playful member of the family that will amuse children and adults alike. It likes the company not only of humans, but also of other cats, with which it will also enjoy playing.

The Siberian Cat becomes physically full-grown only at around three years old.

The Siberian Cat has a very sweet, exceptionally melodious voice.

354

The Siberian Cat is especially at ease in the outdoors, since it adores nature.

The charming, placid Siberian Cat makes a most agreeable companion.

357

The Siberian Cat is very fond of other cats, and needs their company.

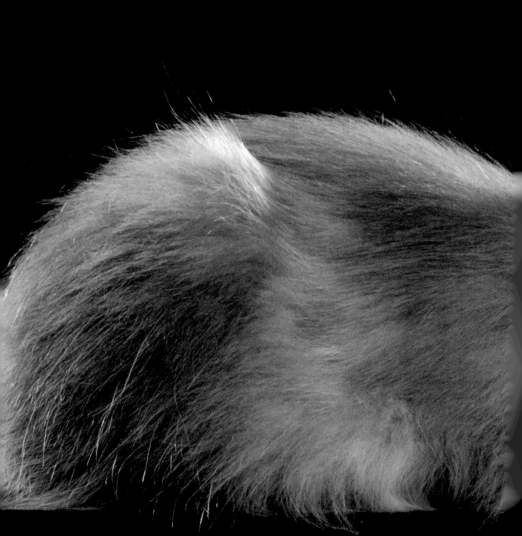

Persians

The Persian owes its charisma and its fame mainly to its long, thick coat, which gives it the appearance of a plush toy. It is, quite simply, the most famous breed in the world, and one of the most adored cats.

There are various different types of Persians, each of which forms a separate division in Europe: solid, shaded, colorpoint, etc. Little is known of its past, just that it has certainly been in existence for centuries, and is probably descended from the Angora. It

Persian

can be traced back to a very long time ago in Iran and Turkey. In the eighteenth century, the explorer Pietro della Valle took Persians back with him to Italy, where they became very popular with the fashionable and aristocratic elite. Later, they also came to the United Kingdom and to France, where they have been bred since the end of the nineteenth century. But it was not until the beginning of the twentieth century that the breed was officially recognized in England, which came to specialize in this type of cat. The Black Persian, a mysterious, regal animal, attracts the most attention. This is a rare cat, because it is difficult to breed, and is undoubtedly one of the oldest Persians known, along with the Blue Persian. Its coat is a solid, pure black and its eyes are yellow or orange, like those of the Bicolor Black and White Persian. The White Persian, also called the French Persian, should have blue

eyes, although other colors are also possible. The Blue Persian, the most sought-after, has a coat that is actually more of a gray color. Recently, breeders have, with great difficulty, succeeded in developing a Persian with a red coat, exotic and beautiful, but quite rare—as is the Cream Persian, which is also extremely beautiful.

The Persian has a serene personality, and is a lovely, easy-going animal.

The Persian gets on very well with people, and also with other cats.

The Persian is mainly an indoor cat, and the stability of the domestic environment is very important to it.

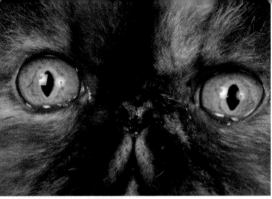

Contrary to preconceptions, beneath its nonchalant exterior the Persian is a lively cat.

The English are without a doubt the best breeders of Persians in the world.

The eyes of the Persian often match its coat color very well.

379

I n 1880 Mrs. Vallence, a British breeder, developed the Persian Chinchilla breed, which was hailed by experts as a great genetic success. It was created by crossing a Silver Tabby Persian with a Smoke Persian.

The first, now legendary, Chinchilla was called Silver Lambkin. It stole the hearts of cat-lovers at the shows. Breeders produced the present-day Chinchilla by breeding this cat with white, blue-eyed Persians. They were exported to the United States, and then at the beginning of the twentieth

peeks a brick-red nose, also edged with black. Like all other Persians, the Chinchilla is a very calm animal that takes very well to the indoor life.

Connoisseurs also favor two other Persians which are very similar to the Chinchilla: the Golden Shaded and the Silver Shaded. The characteristics of the Golden Shaded are the same as those of the Chinchilla, except that its apricot-colored (sometimes even red) coat is very different from the pure white of the Chinchilla. The black tipping affects only one-third of its coat. The Silver Shaded is even more like the Chinchilla, since its coat is white and the tipping is more prominent.

Chinchilla and Golden Shaded

century they began to spread in Europe. The Chinchilla is admired for its silver-white coat with fine "tipping" (black pigmentation of the tips of the hairs of parts of the Chinchilla's coat) evenly distributed over the back, flanks, head, ears, and tail. Its eyes are green and rimmed with black, like well-applied eyeliner. Out of its round head

The Golden and Silver Shaded meow less than the Chinchilla, but otherwise they are all very similar in many respects.

382

The Golden Shaded has one of the most beautiful coats of all, with apricot-colored pigmentation.

The meowing of the Chinchilla is never overpowering; it has such a sweet and melodious tone.

The name Tabby is derived from the name of a type of oriental silk imported by merchants from Baghdad to Britain, a striped cloth known as "attabi." The word "tabby," a description which has spread to all breeds, thus denotes a Persian with a spotted (Spotted Tabby), marbled (Blotched Tabby), or flamed (Mackerel Tabby) coat resembling these silk fabrics.

A large number of coat colors are permitted, such as blue, brown, red, or silver, zones of uniform color contrasting with each other to give the tabby its specific appearance. This type of Persian first appeared at a show in 1871. The Colorpoint Persian is now regarded as a separate breed in America and called the "Himalayan." The rather curious idea of creating a new breed by crossbreeding two cats fundamentally so very different as the Persian and the Siamese occurred to American and English breeders during the 1930s. They wanted to produce a cat that would combine the long hair characteristic of the Persian with the colorpoint pattern of the Siamese. The colors most commonly found are lilac, chocolate, and blue, although in fact some thirty colors are possible. The Himalayan owes its renown above all to its eyes: deep blue, very large, bright, and hypnotic. It is a successful combination of its parents in terms of its appearance, and the same goes for its personality. From the Siamese it gets its stubbornness and energy, from the Persian its

Tabby and Colorpoint (Himalayan) Persians

tranquility and affectionate nobility. This inner duality makes it a sometimes unpredictable, demanding cat.

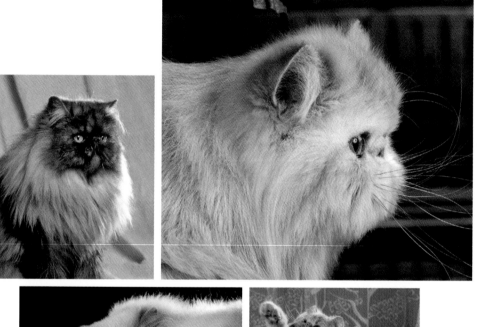

In Persians, the tabby characteristics are often not very pronounced.

The coloring of its very light coat, a beautiful creamy white, resembles that of the Siamese and has colored points on the tail, legs, ears, and face.

The colorpoint pigmentation only appears after a year to 18 months.

The Longhaired Colorpoint was recognized in 1955 in Britain and in 1957, as the Himalayan, in the United States.

399

The Himalayan has a flexible personality and can easily adapt to family life.

The Himalayan needs meticulous grooming because of its long hair.

The World
of the Cat

Paris is frequently associated with that enigmatic, affectionate figure, the tomcat: urban adventurer and freeloader. However, it is undeniably true, strange as it may seem, that our friend the cat has apparently bid farewell to the streets of the French capital.

We seek, we search, we hunt in vain. Perhaps they are just hiding from us out of shyness or wildness, or perhaps on the express orders of their owners who increasingly keep them indoors. The luckiest, or at any rate the most observant, of us may perhaps come across the odd one, all on its own, looking lost, somewhere in a forgotten corner, in a typical old neighborhood that retains the soul of old Paris—perhaps in a quiet backstreet in Ménilmontant, a still-charming cul-de-sac in Montmartre, a grassy area, or a hallowed graveyard. But although the city's authorities claim they have a sizeable community of stray cats under their protection, you would almost think there were no cats left in Paris.

And yet . . . in photographs, postcards, illustrations, films, and legendary places (such as Le Chat Noir, the famous Montmartre nightclub), there is no shortage of signs and evidence of them. Colette, Cartier-Bresson, Doisneau have sung their praises and done their portraits.

Cats, ghostly reflections of a hidden—some would say lost—Paris, seem to belong to the frozen picture of a city of earlier times—the times of the films of Louis Feuillade, in which Irma Vep, rebellious heroine of Vampires, leapt from roof to roof and kept

Cats in Paris

company with the nocturnal cats that this thief happened upon during her wanderings . . .

In Paris, cats are now only seen in a few particular places, such as here in the Père Lachaise cemetery.

409

Alternately downtrodden and affectionate, the cat seems to be in its element in the city.

411

Cats are very much a part
of the scenery, for those
who know where to look.

413

Cats summon up a Paris of nostalgia and colorful fantasy.

Paris is both the backdrop and the stage for cats on the roam.

Cats adore the Parisian parks and gardens where they spend most of their time. They love foraging around there and sometimes, in the case of strays, they even spend the night there.

What would best define the cat? This is a difficult question . . . but the first thing that springs to mind is its playfulness, which it never loses, not even as an adult.

Cats, symbolic as they are of independence, are difficult to put into rigid categories. They cannot easily be pigeon-holed—that would cripple their profound nature, weaken their mystery and magic, and their elusive, unfathomable character. But if we really want to try to describe their fundamental essence, even if only incompletely, then we can point to what all cats always have in common: their love of playing.

It is said of cats that they are creatures of play, that they perform tricks with objects. Amusing themselves is virtually second nature to them; indeed it is a necessity, a duty. Certainly, it is when they are playing that cats seem to blossom most. They love to hide, scratch, jump, climb, camouflage themselves, attack objects, romp, tease,

Cats at Play

nibble." Being good acrobats, they are simply the best at running and jumping. They can make use of most objects and will grab at anything that comes within paw's reach. The most trifling thing can distract them and keep them amused for hours: a ball, a piece of string, a ball of wool, or a wadded-up piece of paper. What is more, their natural elegance is enhanced by their speed and agility.

Cats are in fact pre-programmed to play. In doing so, they are actually practicing their hunting skills. Cats are predestined to kill the mice they play with. Out of this instinct they become creatures of play, and cat-owners should encourage this natural behavior, with toys serving as surrogates.

Anything that moves will arouse the senses of the cat, which will then show itself to be indefatigable in play.

424

Cats are renowned for their agility and their antics. They are exceptionally nimble, whether on four feet or on two.

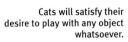
Cats will satisfy their desire to play with any object whatsoever.

Playing enables cats to develop their agility.

430

Playing also enables cats to practice their hunting skills.

S ome myths and clichés are long-lived, such as those regarding the cat's supposed relationships with other animals.

Cats tend to be regarded as antisocial creatures: egocentric, unable to form bonds with any being is different from themselves. Worse still, there is much mention of conflict and of rivalry with the notorious opposition between cats and dogs held up as the ultimate, shining example of this theory. But at best this is only a theory, a preconception. In fact, cats possess the rare talent and the great intelligence to be able to demarcate their environment with great precision and sensitivity, and in doing so they are able to live in harmony with those around them, from whom they receive much affection.

Provided they are not set against each other by a malicious owner, cats and dogs can get along together superbly well and can complement each other, so to speak, with empathy and friendship. Almost 60 % of people who have a cat also have a dog, and that says it all. This does not mean that there are not sometimes tensions between them, but for the most part they live peacefully alongside each other, provided their owner intervenes firmly and fairly in any conflict. Some cats have even been known to defend man's best friend against other cats.

One more observation: despite the fact that cats may sometimes be great predators, especially of birds and rodents, they can also be very caring for them. There are countless anecdotes of chicks being

Cats and Other Animals

rescued by cats attracted by their distressed cheeping.

Although cats are able to live perfectly well alongside other animals, they sometimes show themselves to be formidable predators.

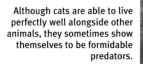

The war between cat and dog is very often just a myth, and is regularly contradicted by reality.

Grooming is one of a cat's
main activities—it has even
become something of a cliché.

Cats keep themselves incredibly clean. True to their free, independent nature, they wash themselves, devoting at least a third of their waking hours to grooming.

They learn this habit from their mothers; it forms an essential part of the rearing of kittens, which will sometimes in turn lick their mothers clean. By washing, they regulate their body temperature and take in small quantities of vitamin D. They also do it to get rid of the scent of humans. More conviction. They look like contortionists, the way they examine every part of their body so meticulously.

However, they do sometimes need help from humans, with their brushes and cloths, if only for the places they cannot reach. It goes without saying that long-haired cats require more frequent grooming than shorthaired cats, since their coats get tangled more quickly. When they wash, they sometimes swallow hair, which forms a ball

Cats and Their Grooming Habits

than just an important ritual, it also gives them an opportunity to withdraw into themselves, to take some time out. Often they will even wash each other, which not only ensures the necessary hygiene, but also creates bonds, making it easier for them to become part of a group and make friendships. Their main grooming tool is their tongue. They constantly lick their coat, paws, and tail painstakingly and with in their stomachs and blocks their digestive tract. It is therefore advisable to brush them every day. Shorthaired cats can get by with a weekly brushing.

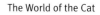

As well as its tongue, a cat will also use its teeth, claws, and paws to wash itself.

Cats are not terribly fond of water, but baths, provided they are not too frequent, may nevertheless be very useful.

Cats have, from time immemorial, been the companions and privileged previewers of artists, and have a status that other animals might envy: a source of inspiration. That is why in all branches of the arts there are incredible numbers of cats to be found in all possible forms.

In ancient Egypt cats were associated with the divine and were evoked through numerous depictions and drawings of Bastet, the goddess of motherhood and procreation. In eighteenth century Japan, Maneki-neko, a terracotta cat with raised paw, was a symbol of good luck. Many writers have based poems and novels on cats: Baudelaire, Edgar Allen Poe, Colette, Joachim de Bellay, Théophile Gautier, Victor Hugo, and Charles Perrault and his Puss in Boots . . . And there are many, many more. In countless Renaissance paintings, and works of later artists, like Ingres, Manet, Suzanne Valadon, and Paul Klee, the cat seems to play an essential, structural role, even if it is not always the main subject. Films, moreover, are not far behind. Children have poignant memories of Disney cartoons, especially *The Aristocats*, the colorful adventures of a family of lovable cats. Cartoon strips should also not be forgotten; for instance "Garfield." And the same goes for the profusion of postcards and postage stamps depicting our friend in all conceivable situations, a source of delight to collectors of all kinds.

Cats in Art

le chat noir

devide..les..ner..fauven..pelote

HEBDOMADAIRE 25 CENTIMES

Left: Rodolphe Salis, founder of the nightclub Le Chat Noir, wrote a literary review in 1882 that paid tribute to the sparkling atmosphere of his establishment.

Below: Cats are often used in advertising.

SCÈNES DE LA VIE DES BÊTES
COLLECTION DIRIGÉE PAR ELIAN-J. FINBERT

CHATS
DE
COLETTE

« M'émerveillerai-je jamais assez des bêtes »
COLETTE

16 HORS TEXTE
EN HÉLIO

ÉDITIONS
ALBIN MICHEL

EXPOSITION FÉLINE INTERNATIONALE
LE CONCOURS DE CHATS DU "JOURNAL"
AU
JARDIN D'ACCLIMATATION
Les 25, 26 et 27 Septembre 1896

SAVON
LE CHAT
EXTRA PUR GARANTI
C. Ferrier & Cie
MARSEILLE

458

Prochainement

TOURNÉE DU CHAT NOIR DE RODOLPHE SALIS

1. Original cover of Colette's book on cats.
2. Poster for the first international cat show in the Jardin d'Acclimatation in Paris.
3, 6 and 7. The cat, central to countless advertisements, seems to have inspired great French soap brands and Californian lemons produced by Sunkist.
4. Picture postcard for a cat-lover.
5. Le Chat Noir in Montmartre, Paris owes its fame partly to this celebrated poster.

459

460

Writers and artists have devoted themselves
wholeheartedly to glorifying the cat
in advertisements and theatre posters.

461

Index